TALKING TO STRANGERS

T0273348

Talking

to

Strangers

RHEA TREGEBOV

THE POETRY IMPRINT AT VÉHICULE PRESS

Published with the generous assistance of the Canada Council for the
Arts and the Canada Book Fund of the Department of
Canadian Heritage.

SIGNAL EDITIONS EDITOR: CARMINE STARNINO

Cover design by David Drummond
Photo of the author by Belle Ancell
Set in Minion and Filosofia by Simon Garamond
Printed by Rapido Books

Dépôt légal, Library and Archives Canada and the
Bibliothèque national du Québec, second trimester 2024

Library and Archives Canada Cataloguing in Publication
Title: Talking to strangers / Rhea Tregebov.
Names: Tregebov, Rhea, 1953- author.
Identifiers: Canadiana (print) 20240310241 | Canadiana (ebook)
2024031025X | ISBN 9781550656565
(softcover) | ISBN 9781550656602 (EPUB)
Subjects: LCGFT: Poetry.
Classification: LCC PS8589.R342 T35 2024 | DDC C811/.54—dc23

Published by Véhicule Press, Montréal, Québec, Canada
vehiculepress.com

Distribution in Canada by LitDistCo
litdistco.ca

Distribution in the U.S. by Independent Publishers Group
ipgbook.com

Printed in Canada on FSC certified paper.

In memory of my sister,
Lee Anne Block

Contents

WHAT WE ARE LEFT

What We Are Left

They didn't want you to be alone. To keep you company, your family
buried miniature terracotta vases, glass pots for healing oils, balms.
And provisions for the travel ahead: half a pig, three hams, cuts of pork,
two chickens. Your brother or sister gave a milk tooth, set on a dish,
childish wish. And your puppy, a curl tendered at your feet. Its collar fitted
with bronze ornaments, a small bell – jingling accompaniment
to your steps in death as in life. But did you ever walk on those feet? Or
was all your travel in their arms, small soul, button-face, mite? No
balm, no healing oil to salve a grief 2000 years long, 2000 years old.

Choral Reef

A pine siskin gorging at the suet
feeder. Pigs snuffling truffles.
Your teacher rapping on the desk
for the class's attention. Dad
subsiding into the sofa at the close
of a long day. Tubas farting.
The soundtrack confounds, this dis-
cordant music of a living reef.

You thought fish were mum. But all this
is the tap-tap of a bully-boy clownfish,
lord of its proprietary anemone,
clanging its teeth to let an underling
know who's boss. The high hoot
of an Ambon damselfish, legendary
for its gumption, as it claims its turf.
This commotion the bustle of
commerce among creatures caught
by the researchers' equipment.

Reef restoration, reparation for the damage
done by dynamite-fishing, humans doing
what they do, then trying to undo
it. Setting hexagonal *reef stars*,
modular metal frames, onto the rubble fields,
making hives coral bits can cling to.

And they do. The fish and their chatter
witness to a reef revived – thanks to
money from Mars (candy
company, not planet). Though
some sounds baffle even the researchers –
these loud clowns, dominatrix damsels
only part of the voluble circus.

The rest we are free to imagine. Kudos
to the Martians: even if we don't buy it,
we do have this scaffolding, this sweet
framework bits of hope cling to,
imagining better.

Metal Fatigue

You wouldn't think the inanimate would get tired
but it does. The ironing board doesn't even sigh
before it collapses and I'm left like Wile E. Coyote,
treading air, the iron aloft in my hand, my hand held
on the plane where I expected a surface to be. Steel
can't bend, so it breaks. Or it bends and bends, bit
by bit moving towards the moment it surrenders.
No wonder it didn't sigh. No one wants to listen to you
complain. Nobody wants to know how tired you are.

Swainson's Thrush

Happy for the light,
their voices woke me
in the spring dawn.

And here, your small body, perfect,
on the sidewalk beside the drugstore.
Body someone soon will sweep away,
dump or place in a bin, caring or careful or
careless.

Wall

Tired, a bit unsteady, I lean
against you, moss giving
underneath my hand. Moss a small
cosmos of valleys and peaks, nations
of trees and shrubs, countries of ferns
and vines. What's a wall to do?
Hold earth so we're not buried, water
so we're not drowned. Keep the good
from the bad. Hold a flood,
landslide of those who want to be
on our side, want to be where
we are, where we don't want them.

Place

The simplest things
elude me.
What was the life I had.

Today I don't
know where I stand: by a quirk
of the weather it's one season

on one side of the street,
another on the other. Hedges
greening into May to the north,

snow huddling in January
to the south. If I cross this street,
I might be halfway across the country,

today might be yesterday and I
the girl waiting for her life.
If I cross this street, I might

be halfway across the world, today
might be tomorrow, and I
a woman waiting for

the siege to end with nothing
in her arms
but her bleeding son.

The End of Everything

Cosmology knows everything began
(remember the Big Bang?) and will
end. Stars form, die; galaxies morph.
The universe won't stay. The astrophysicist
figures we have five paths: Heat Death,
Big Crunch, Big Rip, Vacuum Decay or,
finally, my personal favourite, Bouncing
Cosmologies. Contrary to popular
opinion, Heat Death is in fact the death
of heat, not death *by* heat – this big chill
is the most likely suspect. For the Big
Crunch, picture a classic house of cards –
Twin Towers pancaking. Everything we can
imagine and all we can't folding inwards
into itself. The Big Rip is plain rage: dark
energy, which we don't understand, at war
with the stuff we do: stars torn from
galaxies (poor stars), planets (poor
planets) torn from their stars till everyone
is alone in their own dimming little
pool of light. Vacuum Decay
has the universe shudder, succumb
to a basic instability, giving in
to some core flaw. I do like the unlikely
Bouncing Cosmologies, where every
thing pinballs, beginning and ending
cycling over and over and over again. Some
comfort there. When the astrophysicist is asked
what this has to do with us, she says we are

irrelevant, inconsequential. Perfectly
insignificant. So what do we have to do
with this if *we* don't matter? What
is the end of everything, in particular,
us? Maybe this, maybe for us, this: *everything*
may be one countenance, one single look or,
in these days of pestilence, touch. Someone
we know like the back of our hand, that
someone touching our hand. These are
days of pestilence, days of "excess deaths,"
every day each death a death too many,
each death the end of a world.

TALKING TO STRANGERS

Talk: White Night

Whitehorse, Yukon, June 2011

We're all strangers in the startling light
of midnight, but we seat ourselves beside
the young woman in the dim booth in the bar, talk
about the light, the dark inside. The kilometres she's driven
solo from Vancouver with her dogs, sleeping in her van.
She's fine, she says, she's safe with the dogs. She just needed
something – a flinch in her mouth I catch. To get away.

Talk drifts to the hockey riots ten days ago,
when the Canucks lost the big game. Fans
segued into mob, began their labours
tipping Porta Potties, garbage cans, moved on
to torching police cars, trashing pizza joints. Then
anything. Now, inside the bar's dull light we watch
ten-day-old footage on someone's phone, smoke
rolling thick as silk on sidewalks the angry men
own for a bit. *I need a weapon,*
a sweet-faced boy says, watching another
crack his skateboard against a car.
And it's work to break through the tough glass.
When at last they win, watchers cheer, take
trophy snapshots, videos: victory Vs,
triumphant poses. There have been walls between
them and what they want, their team has failed,
so now they'll take walls down, fill their arms
with things they don't have or don't have enough of.

25

I was there, the young woman tells us. She's
a paramedic. That night she was out with the cops,
the people she'd come to help hurt her.
She pushes back her bangs to show the bruise.
She's safe with the dogs. She just needed to get away.
Beyond the windows the sun broods
over the horizon, not ready to go.

Talk: IDF

Tel Aviv–Haifa, March 2018

At the station, the world's smallest
soldier gives up her seat for me on the slow
train to Haifa. Other than *thank you*, I don't know
what to say. All the long way she leans
against the baggage rack, her head
not grazing its railing. Jostled, scrolling
her phone, watching American cooking shows
in miniature. She looks good in khaki.
You wouldn't think they made uniforms
that size, but it fits. The Uzi (rate of fire
600 rounds per minute) fits too. All the young
soldiers look at home with their fresh weapons,
knapsacks. As we near Haifa, I thank her again,
two hours on her feet instead of me. She tells me
it's her job. It's a soldier's job to give up seats
to older women on trains, to admonish others
in strict Hebrew to give up theirs. She's from
New Jersey, she says; been here two years. Didn't know
a word of Hebrew. She's a volunteer. Isn't it hard,
in combat, not knowing the language well? In combat
it isn't hard. You just go where the others go,
do what they do. She was in Nablus, it was
rough, they're letting her out early. She'll stay
in Haifa, she says, find a place to live.
Her hand steady on the Uzi.

Talk: Luck

Quadra Island, BC, August 2019

We're lucky here. Our cabins aren't fancy but they are
pricey. And though the Amazon, Alaska, Siberia
are aflame, we have no wildfire smoke this year.
We meet near the dock, this tall calm woman, and
she tells me how her husband died, fourteen months ago.
A left shoulder sore from swimming, they thought.
So she stopped the car, and they stood beside
the blaze of traffic while she placed her capable hands
where she thought the pain was. As he got back in,
he buckled, folded into himself. She's trained,
did CPR for 20 minutes but he was gone. She has
to tell this story. The seven years she had with him.
The long wait till they met. Now she's back working
with kids in trauma and it's good. This is her first vacation.
When she was invited here by friends, it felt right.
Though it's hard to be with people who didn't know
her husband because it's hard to explain him to people
who didn't know him. But she has to tell me,
who just met her. Has to tell everyone.

Talk: Sidewalk

Toronto, October 2019

The man bleeding won't sit down. He'll hold
the towel the bystander got him from the nail salon
tight around his wrist, and he'll raise his arm
above his head like we ask him but he won't sit down.
He's sad about the six-pack that fell and cut him,
sad they're broken. And it hurts where the glass sliced
but he won't sit on the curb. My son has called 911
and we want the ambulance to come, we want
the siren wailing towards us because the blood scares us
brightening the white towel with red, the new one,
second one, that the bystander, a young woman
with a backpack, thinking quick, has also fetched. Blood
shines on the sidewalk, on the street. The man bleeding
is tall, tall as my son, and we're afraid of how
far he could fall. His speech isn't quite right, and
he's angry when my son tells the dispatcher
he might be intoxicated. *I have a brain injury*,
he tells us. *I was in a car accident twelve years
ago. I was in a wheelchair for two years.
I apologize*, my son says. *I made a mistake.
It's okay*, the man says. *You made a mistake.*
But he won't sit down. *I've sat enough*, he says.

Talk: Tourists

Havana, Cuba, December 2019

No fourth wall to breach on these streets: through
open windows, doors, small dramas overlap,
intersect: people spoon soup, iron shirts, watch soaps. Pale
obvious couple in sturdy shoes, we're open too.
Taxi? Do we need a taxi? Are we hungry, thirsty?
Questions flicker, flicked. What do we think of Cuba
the gaunt man in the brilliant white shirt asks
as music sidles from a bar. His grimace at our rote reply.
What do we know? Where are we from
asks the lean gent in the brown sportscoat. Canada,
his opinion of Canada is good, as is his friend's.
We shake hands, introduce ourselves, poised
on the sidewalk to part, which
we do. Our flight home direct.

Talk: Karma

Vancouver, February 2020

The virus is distant, we're at the airport.
The man across from us, heavy-bellied
in a stained white T-shirt, notices my glance and
smiles, tells us he's been flying 18 hours. *Karma*,

he tells us, his hands steering a circle that
swivels this way and then that. His sister first
won a million-dollar lottery, then had a stroke.
The hospital in Manila wanted $7000 to admit her.
He's glad he lives in this country. He tells us

his father died 20, no, 10 years ago. He felt
then that a man should not cry but he did cry.
He dreams still of his father, his father
driving a convertible with the top down, saying,
come with me. His father never owned a car,
didn't know how to drive. What does it mean?
He's not young anymore, he knows. We check

our watches, our flight is leaving we tell him,
we tell him goodbye, decline his offered hand.

Talk: Scrap

Winnipeg, August 2020

Across the kitchen table my cousin – whose life at a distance
seemed to contain extravagances (white couches, white
pooches, white rugs) – tells me she doesn't want to waste.
I've witnessed her cakes with their delectable flourishes,
her T-bones broiled medium-rare, dessert-aperitif confections.
But now she wants to use all her odds and sods, orts, every
scrap: the tan bones of chicken carcass, honey-coloured onion
skins, freckled potato peels, curls of carrot parings, ferny fronds
of carrot tops, pale green celery stalk furls. Things I throw
into a bucket to rot. She has a diagnosis, doesn't talk prognosis.
She's making stock. Frozen, it keeps for months. She's thinking
past this fall into winter, its short days. Taking stock.

Talk: Detox

Vancouver, January 2021

I'm pacing the long lonesome
winter shoreline again; soft
grey sand, clouds, sky. The virus
still with us. Careful greetings
for the odd dog, owner, masked
and unmasked. A variant from
my usual path takes me down
to the water where a young woman
in a hoody hugs her knees, watches
waves touch and withdraw, touch
and withdraw. Six feet between us,
we chat up the ordinary.
She also changed course, wanted
a run, then had to stop to sit where
it's peaceful. I gabble on about
running, gravel versus concrete.
She smiles, then her hands open,
her face switches. She tells me
she just heard from a friend. He's gone
and left detox two days before
he would have qualified for rehab.
Toxic drugs something else that's
killing us, killing so many more of us
here in this beautiful grey winter, though
it's something we think we can blame
on those dead. She wishes he'd stayed.
It's scary, I tell her. I know

people who've died, OD'd.
We care and care and can
only do so much, and that much
isn't enough. She wishes she
could do more.

Talk: Tangle

Gibson's, BC, June 2021

I'm on the patio of a small-town West Coast cafe,
where an ancient hippie with a Southern drawl
runs bejewelled fingers through her long grey curls
as she espouses her philosophy of life. Which is this,
or that. *Wise nods, man, wise nods.* She's not talking to me
and I don't want to tangle with her. Instead sit
in judgement as sparrows gather for crumbs
among the smugness, the psychobabble. *Just   breathe*
she breathes. The stilted intonations. She may
or may not believe in vaccines, so I sit
at a healthy distance. Now she is telling her friends
about looking after her dying father. It was bad.
Tells them about the cottage where she nursed him,
the clutter, the clusterfuck of feelings she had.
The way she felt she had to sort the many fishing rods
stored there, their lines a jumble. The harder
she tried, the worse it got. Her son J., *he's a real trip, man.*
J. Yeah. He came out onto the porch, the crazy cat's cradle
of fishing lines she'd spawned stopping him. He went back
into the cottage, came out with scissors. *No, man, no,*
she told him. He cut till the tangles opened. *It's over,*
he told her, went back inside. She puts her face in her hands.
I run bare fingers through my curls.

Talk: Mask

Winnipeg, February 2022

I've left you, what's left of you, in palliative care,
am walking the frigid sidewalks to find lunch, my face
masked against the cold and the virus. A big
man, his own face masked, comes towards me
and as we pass, fake-coughs, growls: *I have Covid.*
His face inches from mine. All my anger choking, I turn
to chase after him, shout, *What did you say? What
did you say to me?* The small man behind him,
who must be his friend, turns to face me with his
own masked face. *My sister is dying of cancer
and you mock me?* I scream. The friend stretches
his arms to the side, palms up. Signals me to stop.
He's not mocking you, he tells me. *He's sick.
He's just sick.* His palms up, protecting me,
his friend. *OK,* I tell him. *OK. Thanks.* And turn.
I can do nothing for you, beyond protection, but care.

HOW IT WORKS

How It Works

Though I don't know how planes work
I fly. This miracle, a thing we've made. Trust
is necessary or we crash. I thought love
was a thing, some thing I could touch with my hands

like a chair or a table; my sister's knuckle, husband's wrist
a miracle. But nothing is a thing. Not things, not thought.
Everything is motion, backwards or forwards, crashing,
recombining: my husband's body beside someone

else's now, sister's in earth. I also lie beside another body,
beside a mind I can't touch, one that knows process, being,
subatomic bits of matter, that understands how things work.
I want to say to this man: let your body trust me, tell me

about your loneliness, about the boy you fail to describe,
boy alone in the kitchen, spooning beans from a can
to his wanting mouth, hungering. Tell me why you're bereft
if I turn from your body in the night – and yet you want

your loneliness untended, preserved. Trust, you say, is dangerous –
we know what people do. But we don't need love to be a thing
we can put our hands on to trust. Trust me, you; believe
that we know the miracle, how it works.

Second Generation

You want to keep everything. Obsolete dust-encrusted
plastic-wrapped blank mini-cassettes for the defunct video
camera that caught the kids' lives. Vacant jewel cases
that don't hold any of the music you don't play. To save
everything: the tin can long parted from its label that might
hold something good. The '80s sweatshirt, fluorescent
logo rusting flake by plastic flake into cipher. To keep
everything you never had: that real live monkey orphaned
in its teacup the back pages of the comic book offered
for the little you couldn't afford. Just one glance from the girl
practising flute in the girls' bathroom, its lonesome tones not
for you. To save everything the War took: your father's
mother, his father, side-by-side; her lace collar, white
blouse pressed, his suit solemn, dark. Unknowable uncles,
aunts, cousins, their faces in photos on no wall.

Refuah

The first time you kissed me
an even dozen years ago
in your beautiful house
looking out over the garden,
the water,
the mountains,
and held me,
a grown woman
who had travelled
to where I found you
mostly past hope,
I laid my head against your chest
and said: *you feel like home.*

And when I said *home*
I must have thought of places I knew –
my last city, where in the bustle,
every call has its response.
Or the place I grew up in,
prairie that might welcome anyone.

But perhaps home with you
is ancestral, the land
of Israel, a place of milk
and honey, olive groves.
The land we're travelling in,
where I keep asking
what words mean and you keep
knowing. Israel, which is

also Palestine. A land fractured,
the land, maybe, where you live,
where there is always war. Home

where you stay
armed and ready. Because
you come from a hard place
I never lived, where I live
sometimes with you. I ask
if *refuah* in Hebrew means *remedy*
and you tell me *healing.*

March 2018

Step

No daughter of mine, this girl,
yours. All that cuddling, coddling,
all that kept her what she was: brat,
petulant gangster thugging her way
through breakfasts of prefab
oatmeal, lunches of bunny-shaped
mac n' cheese. Her palate, as I
predicted on meeting her, spoiled.
Why don't you just feed her pablum?
I moaned and you, her father, my lover,
for your sins, laughed. Years I played
fifth wheel circling the family ruins,
and her the angel avenging her mother's
hurt. Years she outstripped me, five foot ten.
Stripped me, blabbermouth that I am,
even of words, keeping *my mouth
shut* about affairs that you told me
were *none of my business.*
Not mine, this girl, whom
I badmouthed to my own
kin. Shame on me. But the hapless
love I had, have for her, girl now
grown, exquisite, brainy, funny.
This girl of my hapless heart,
would I ever give her up, give up
on her? No. Daughter of mine.

Singing Away the Bears

You're ahead of me on the trail.
You don't talk. Don't
mind the singing. I know
I don't measure up
to the woman you'd want:
quick, brave.
The bears are real.
Even when they're not
near. Even when they are
neither, with or without
you, I do this. Raise
my voice, lift it through fear.

Definition

I describe my woes to my friend, the pro, genius
of a plot greater and finer than my own big old garden
where everything grows into everything else. *Definition,*
she tells me. That's what I need. I was defined

by a cold place, a time when summer was brief and
brilliant. By a house of enough in a neighbourhood
of just- and not-enough. Pink petunias and orange marigold,
a red rose or two. But here, too much. Too much moneywort

invaded by stonecrop inveigled by barrenwort entangled
with leopard's bane. Besotted, greedy, jealous
to save every bloom, leaf, for me this more than
enough isn't too much. Can't yank a stem

I call flower not weed. Though there is
the buttercup war I keep waging, kneeling
on stones like a penitent, cursing their stubborn
fecund being. *But what's the difference between*

flowers and weeds? Peter, at eight, enlisted as foot soldier,
asks. *Pull everything up and what comes back
is weed,* my dad in his heyday would kid, neatly
defining invasive. Define need. Define enough.

My friend tells me I need to learn to say no
to ferns sprouting in the daylilies, to sweet woodruff
infiltrating hosta. Need to define what it is I want,
what I keep, love, let flourish. I want too much.

Consent

Because it's July, despite a winter those of us in this mild
clime called harsh, because I watered and weeded, and the bees,
despite their losses, did their work, so that the raspberries act
as an education in bounty, and because I can't abide
waste, especially in this world hungry for food, and beauty,
twice a day, morning and early evening, I go outside to gather.
Because of this plenty, I am picking only those berries
that yield to me, those whose coral is turning to purple,
the ones a gentle tug releases from their white core,
which holds, or the ones that simply fall into my palm.
I say the berries yield, are ripe, but berries are not women
and women not berries. I don't know what berries want,
to propagate I suppose, but they don't want in the same way
women do, who are not ripe or not according to the picker's eye,
who are not plucked, though they may pluck themselves.
I live with a man who can be lying beside me taut with want
and who will, at a word or a touch, because I am angry or
tired or sad, stop. Because it's easy for me to calmly compare
women to berries and do violence to neither.

WHAT WE DO

What My Body Did

Skipped double dutch in the chill spring
playground, galoshes whomping;
turned lopsided somersaults, but not
cartwheels. Rolling-pinned down
the dizzy green hill in the park
to sit up and watch the sky whirl. Beat sugar
into beaten butter, the wooden spoon
gold and granulated. Lugged a suitcase
over cobblestoned streets, did sun
salutations naked on the parquet floor
in that college town. Laid itself
across a bed, solemn or glad,
to greet another body, warmth,
that came, and went. Learned hard
to run, a personal best that wasn't
good but good enough, down
concrete, lapping at that song inside,
that keening, till, muted, it murmured
instead of clanged. Made the keyboard
sound like rain, like dancing. Never
once lay in bed all day, no
matter what song or keening
rang inside. Rose and dressed
and went into the kitchen, ran
a cloth under the faucet, wrung it out and
over and back, followed an invisible

path to clean. Clean, that counter,
the floor, windows, even curtains.
Clean, face, hands, whatever
clogged the neural networks in the skull,
soul.   And made you.   It made you.

Voice Mail

I'm going out singing,
my mother's message, voice
I've known all my long life.
It's choir practice, at 92 she still
goes. *I'm going out singing,* she says.
You might not be able to reach me tonight.

Kaddish: Villanelle

According to the custom, I recite the prayer for my father,
though not to any god I know, certainly not the god
of the congregation, the synagogue, I do not understand.

Synagogue my father attended most of his long life, where, the day after
his funeral, my sisters & I are not counted for the necessary ten,
so no prayer is said. According to the custom, I pray for my father

for eleven months, as a comfort, carrying in my woman's purse
the card given at the graveside with the words spelled out on it,
carrying that paper till the edges wear. And though I do not understand

them fully, I come to know the words with all my heart, all my might,
& I say them when I lie down & when I rise up. Saying them,
according to the custom, I hear the gravel & earth of my father's prayers

for his father, his mother, his voice intoning *yis'gadal*, made large, &
yis'kadash, made holy. A large holy prayer to comfort the bewildered
living, meant to honour, even redeem, the dead. I do not understand

this prayer *beyond all blessings, hymns, praises, & consolations
uttered in the world*, by what means it comforts or bewilders or redeems.
And though according to the custom I pray for my father,
& in congregation nod *amen*, I do not understand.

God

I was smug in Grade One, judging the idolators
and their little gods as I learned that first
commandment. I continue smug, sure we're
meat: matter not spirit. Ghosts, souls? – no
perception once the body's abolished.
But, today, caught by an eagle high
above the Pacific, what is the kinship
I feel, the wish to *come back* as one,
fierce, keen, above everything earthly
but of the earth?

Menial

Each time I drench the hydrangeas I have
the day Helen gave me their watery
needs and name. And when in my own kitchen
I drop three popcorn kernels into the pan,
then wait for their exact bursts, I hear John,
patient, tutoring me. *Keep shaking the pan.*
Dave's large capable hands snapping
asparagus stalks for the grill, his knowing
where they want to break. Today I do not
want to slice cremini mushrooms for the quiche
I used to make Nancy. What alchemy
do I expect will feed those who no longer
need food? This is the year I count dead
friends, still count them on one hand.

What We Do

for SG, October 2022

An empty face mask hangs from the doorknob.
Your apartment empty too. I'm watering
plants, taking in mail, things a friend does. You're
at your mother's, doing things a daughter does,
the house empty of her. You don't have
to save her anymore. Not from the virus.
Not from the war she survived. Or her own
body emptying itself of all her strength.
She'd had enough. The law let her do for
herself. One last dinner, all the family
sat at that table, sated, her dead too.

Sunday

for MG 1946 – 2014

Nothing much happened.
Just the usual Sunday. Laundry
folded, she came upstairs. This last bit
of November, sun in and out all day,
but mild, a surprise she liked. No sign
she was sick but that night she'd slept
poorly, pain of some kind
in her stomach. Last spring, she had
the sofa recovered, three serious days spent
picking fabric – flocked or jacquard, tweed
maybe, a quality blend – Mike kidded her about.
We'll be living twenty years with it,
she told him. Planning for Christmas,
her granddaughter's first, planning three months
in Miami, away from all the cold to come,
she lay down, cheek against the floral she had chosen,
for a nap. Sun came out again, ticked
across the carpet, across her feet, chest, face.
Mike came in, an aspirin for her headache,
cup of tea, sugar, no milk. He touched her shoulder.
He thought he'd wake her.

For NR, Her Second Round of Chemo

It's a speck lays me low: some bit of thing
my body refuses – or that refuses
my body – puts me on intimate terms
with the bathroom floor. There is nothing to
appease this nausea; reduced to intake, output,
at least I'm near what I need. I have felt,
now and again, my life sour, but I
can't remember wanting this much to not
be in my body, to shuck flesh. Except
I know for me it will end.

Facts

Elizabeth Taylor is the most
beautiful woman in the world.
She has cornflower-blue eyes.
She lives in a mansion in Hollywood
or New York or Paris. I live
on Matheson Avenue in Winnipeg.
I am not beautiful. I am not a woman.
I'm a girl with plain brown eyes.
I don't know what cornflowers are,
though I do know beauty, their kin,
these backyard bachelor buttons
bending manifold along the fence.

TASTES

Bitter

It's late to learn to know
zest from pith. To navigate
the weight of what
you had and don't
anymore, of losing
what you couldn't
do without. Citrus.
The recipe faded words
pencilled on a torn-out
page of endpaper. The taste
of marmalade on toast,
tang of someone gone
twenty years now. You need
to distinguish between
flavedo and albedo,
between lemon yellow
and the white pulp beneath.
Between what is held
bright in the mouth,
sharp with colour, and what
will grind white and hostile
in your teeth.

Umami

Something was killed
for you, for this. Brown-
eyed, likely, like
you, your tribe. Lashed.
A slice of its life
on your plate. But
your mouth can't hold
its water. What you want,
need. The recipe ripe, ancestral:
garlic, braised in gold
broth. This time
you chose inosinate
over guanylate, brisket
over shiitake. Umami,
the marker for protein,
a word you scarcely
know. You do know
what you chose
you must change.

Salt

It's not you the dog
loves, it's the briny
lick of your skin. What
you loved first. Pickle
to you meant cucumber,
picked from its bristled
prickly stem; one clove
garlic, one sprig dill.
Not just that crunch in
your mouth – the
mineral thirst, slaked.
That taste first taste ever
on your tongue, that
sip of amniotic fluid,
inside out.

Sour

Pucker. That face
either offering
or distaste. Ready
to kiss or spit. Appetite
or aversion. Mild acid
etches your mouth.
Milk that's turned
against you. Or what
you can't get, so
don't want. Or do you
want only what you
can't get, do you want
what hurts? Let's say
you like it mixed,
tempered with sweet.
Lemon pie. Borscht
made with rhubarb
and honey. Let's say
that.

Sweet

Cats don't care, can't
taste it – carnivores, they
don't need energy
without protein. You
don't either but want it.
Would indulge in most
of the seven deadly
to get it, greedy
glutton that you are,
lusting, envious even
of that kid in the
candy store, lazily
chewing his pastel candy
necklace. You remember
the nothing they were
dissolving on the
tongue. That kid's
grin, yes, you'd swap
anything for that.

BEHOLD:
NOTES TOWARDS AN ELEGY

For my sister, Lee Anne Block,
February 9, 1952 – February 19, 2022

1.

I saw the fox.
The squirrel first,
frantic. Then the fox,
stalk stalled. By me.
She looked at me.
Still.

2.

A look that said
hineh. Here is.
Hineni. Here I am.
Behold. Present.

3.

At a distance something
struggling in the grass:
moth, leaf,
bird?

That something, you?

4.

I look for you everywhere:
moth, leaf, bird, fox.

But it was just a fox.
Unlikely. In a Toronto yard.
A real fox. A real
scared squirrel.

Not an omen,
totem.

Enough.

Stupid.

5.

I look for you everywhere.
You. Me.
I never did
understand
the difference.
Until now.

Not now.

Not yet.

6.

I believe your
death no more than
I believe my own,
no less.

7.

You gone
the centre snatched.
Blur, blank I can't
see, can't see past.

8.

Grief here
not you.

You're nowhere
in these words.

9.

Big sister,
mirror, self.

You stood
ahead of,
beside me.
Doorway
to the world.

First.

Bravest.

Fairy-tale wolf under my bed
you chased away.

10.

I had a private
toddler language
only you understood,

my sister tongue.

What did I say?

(*Behold.*
Here I am.)

It was you
who translated me
into the world.

11.

I'm not myself,
not all here.

(Hineni)

And here's the point: you are not you.

12.

So I'm not myself and if I'm not myself
who am I?

You'd say: *if I am not for myself who
is for me?*

13.

And here I am.
Present.
Without you.
How do I keep you
alive inside me?
How do I keep me
alive inside without you?

Behold. Here I am.
Here and not here.
Here it is:
world without you.

14.

That fox stopped.
Held. In my head.
By me. She's not you.
Oh me.
O you.

AUTHOR'S NOTES

"What We Are Left": Reference to a 2021 archaeological discovery in France.

"Choral Reef": From the CBC Radio program *Quirks & Quarks* on reef restoration in Indonesia funded by the Mars Foundation.

"The End of Everything": From the CBC Radio program *Quirks & Quarks* interview with astronomer Katie Mack about her book, *The End of Everything (Astrophysically Speaking)* (2020).

"Place": Vancouver/Ghouta, Syria, February 20, 2018

"Second Generation": A vintage ad for these "almost human" pets referred to in the poem:

"What We Do": Canadian law provides for medical assistance in dying for those who are mentally competent and in an advanced state of decline, experiencing unbearable suffering that cannot be relieved under conditions they consider acceptable.

"Behold": *Hineh* (הנה) is Hebrew for "here is." *Hineni* (הנני) is Hebrew for "here I am." "If I am not for myself who is for me?" is a portion of the philosopher Hillel's famous saying "If I am not for myself, who is for me? And if I am only for myself, what am I? And if not now, when?"

ACKNOWLEDGEMENTS

I want to express my gratitude to my editor, Carmine Starnino, for his continued support for my writing and especially for his eye on these poems, which made for a much better book. Thanks also to Sam Znaimer, Julie Bruck and Adrienne Drobnies, whose wisdom and support helped me through many drafts.

Thanks also to the editors who published the following poems in the following journals: "Provisional" [now titled "Sunday"], *CV 2* 37, no. 4 (Spring 2015); "Sonnet: Nausea." *Juniper* 1, no. 2. Web. (November 2017); "Talk: White Night." *The Walrus* 16, no. 7 (September 2019); "Menial" and "Talk: IDF." *Fiddlehead*, no. 284 (Summer 2020); "Talk: Scrap." *Room* 44, no. 1 (March 2021); "Kaddish," "Metal Fatigue." *HAL (Hamilton Arts and Letters)* 15, no. 2. Web. (2022-23); "Sweet" and "Umami." *Malahat Review,* no. 224 (Fall 2023); "Definition." *The Walrus* 21, no. 1 (January/February 2023).

Talya Rubin • Richard Sanger • Stephen Scobie
Peter Dale Scott • Deena Kara Shaffer
Carmine Starnino • Andrew Steinmetz • David Solway
Ricardo Sternberg • Shannon Stewart
Philip Stratford, trans. • Matthew Sweeney
Harry Thurston • Rhea Tregebov • Peter Van Toorn
Patrick Warner • Derek Webster • Anne Wilkinson
Donald Winkler, trans. • Shoshanna Wingate
Christopher Wiseman • Catriona Wright
Terence Young